LEN DAWSON, PRIEST HOLMES, MACK LEE HILL, OTIS TAYLOR, CARLOS CARSON, TONY GONZALEZ, JOHN ALT, JIM TYRER, ED BUDDE, WILL SHIELDS, JACK RUDNAY, NEIL SMITH, ART STILL, BUCK BUCHANAN, JERRY MAYS, WILLIE LANIER, DERRICK THOMAS, BOBBY BELL, EMMITT THOMAS, ALBERT LEWIS, DERON CHERRY, JOHNNY ROBINSON, NICK LOWERY, JERREL WILSON, LEN DAWSON, PRIEST HOLMES, MACK LEE HILL, OTIS TAYLOR, CARLOS CARSON, TONY GONZALEZ, JOHN ALT, JIM TYRER, ED BUDDE, WILL SHIELDS, JACK RUDNAY, NEIL SMITH, ART STILL

THE STORY OF THE KANSAS CITY CHIEFS

THE STORY OF THE KANSAS CITY CHIEFS

BY JIM WHITING

CREATIVE EDUCATION / CREATIVE PAPERBACKS

PUBLISHED BY CREATIVE EDUCATION AND CREATIVE PAPERBACKS
P.O. BOX 227, MANKATO, MINNESOTA 56002
CREATIVE EDUCATION AND CREATIVE PAPERBACKS ARE IMPRINTS OF THE
CREATIVE COMPANY
WWW.THECREATIVECOMPANY.US

DESIGN AND PRODUCTION BY BLUE DESIGN (WWW.BLUEDES.COM)
ART DIRECTION BY RITA MARSHALL
PRINTED IN CHINA

PHOTOGRAPHS BY AP IMAGES (ASSOCIATED PRESS), GETTY IMAGES (PETER G.
AIKEN, ROBIN ALAM/ICON SPORTSWIRE, VERNON BIEVER/NFL, JAY
BIGGERSTAFF/TUSP, RICH CLARKSON/SI, JONATHAN DANIEL/STRINGER,
STEPHEN DUNN, JAMES FLORES/NFL, FOCUS ON SPORT, GEORGE GOJKOVICH,
ROD HANNA/NFL, TOM HAUCK, ANDY HAYT, WESLEY HITT, DAVID E. KLUTHO/
SI, NFL PHOTOS, DARRYL NORENBERG/NFL, JOE ROBBINS, JAMIE SQUIRE,
DAMIAN STROHMEYER/SI, RON VESELY, SCOTT WINTERS/ICON SPORTSWIRE),
KANSAS CITY PUBLIC LIBRARY (MISSOURI VALLEY SPECIAL COLLECTIONS)

NAMES: WHITING, JIM, AUTHOR.
TITLE: THE STORY OF THE KANSAS CITY CHIEFS / JIM WHITING.
SERIES: NFL TODAY.
INCLUDES INDEX.
SUMMARY: THIS HIGH-INTEREST HISTORY OF THE NATIONAL FOOTBALL
LEAGUE'S KANSAS CITY CHIEFS HIGHLIGHTS MEMORABLE GAMES, SUMMARIZES
SEASONAL TRIUMPHS AND DEFEATS, AND FEATURES STANDOUT PLAYERS SUCH
AS DERRICK THOMAS.
IDENTIFIERS: LCCN 2018035585 / ISBN 978-1-64026-145-7 (HARDCOVER) / ISBN
978-1-62832-708-3 (PBK) / ISBN 978-1-64000-263-0 (EBOOK)
SUBJECTS: LCSH: KANSAS CITY CHIEFS (FOOTBALL TEAM)—HISTORY—JUVENILE
LITERATURE.
CLASSIFICATION: LCC GV956.K35 W47 2019 / DDC 796.332/6409778411—DC23

FIRST EDITION HC 9 8 7 6 5 4 3 2 1
FIRST EDITION PBK 9 8 7 6 5 4 3 2 1

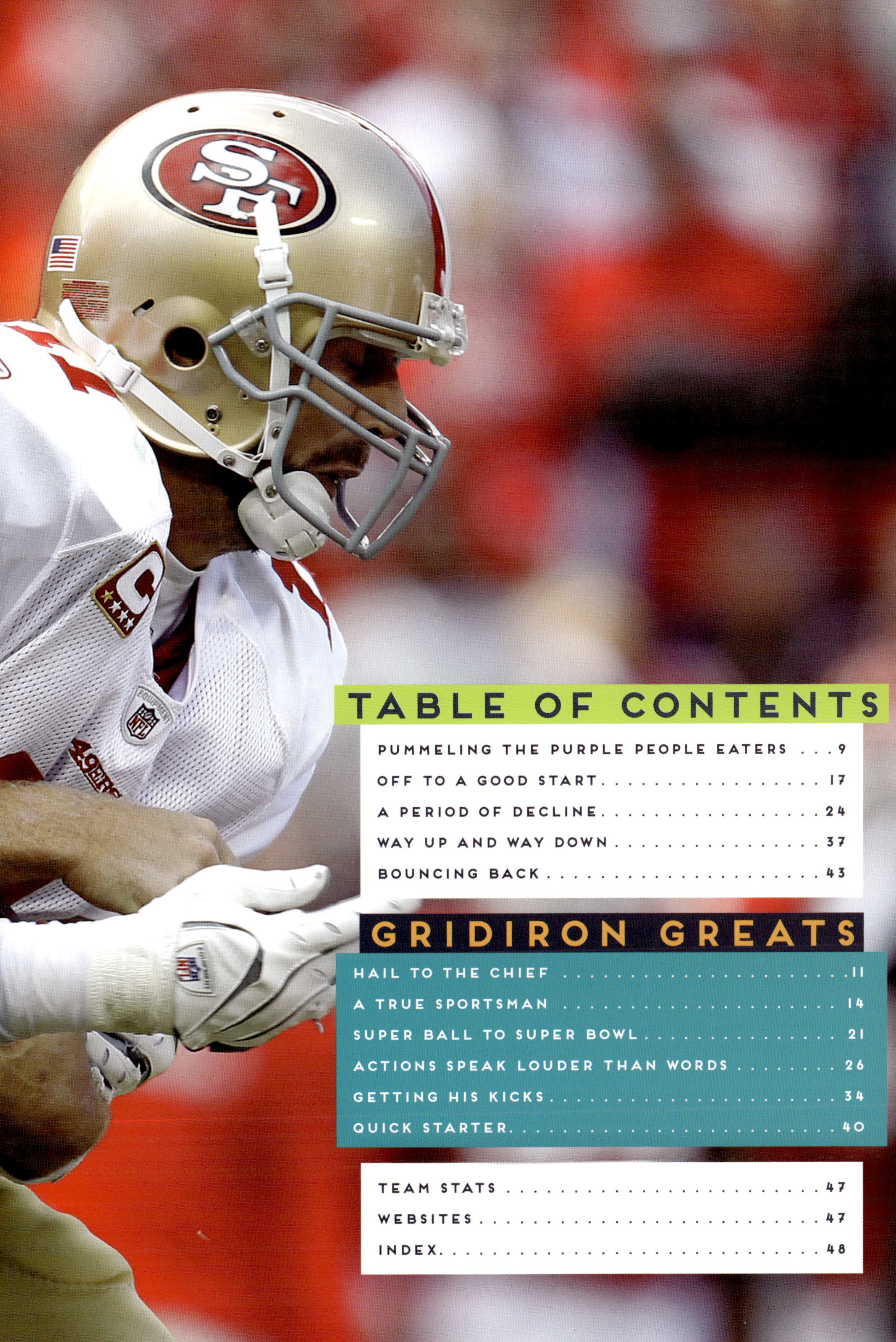

PUMMELING THE PURPLE PEOPLE EATERS

The American Football League (AFL) and National Football League (NFL) agreed to merge in 1966. The NFL was much older. Many people thought that the quality of play in the NFL was higher. They looked to the first two Super Bowls as evidence. Until the merger became official in 1970, the Super Bowl pitted the NFL and AFL champions. The NFL's Green Bay Packers easily won Super Bowl I and II. The AFL's New York Jets raised a few doubts the following year, though. They beat the Baltimore Colts.

The Minnesota Vikings were poised to restore order in Super Bowl IV. They would take on the Kansas City Chiefs. During the regular season, Minnesota had won 12 games in a row. The Vikings led the NFL in points scored. They also allowed the fewest points. The heart of the defense was the line. Those players were nicknamed the "Purple People Eaters." The Vikings wore purple jerseys. "The Purple People Eater" was the title of a popular 1958 song. Minnesota was the overwhelming favorite. This was in part due to the Chiefs' performance in Super Bowl I. The Packers had crushed them, 35–10.

The Chiefs hadn't even won their division in 1969. People said they were sneaking into Super Bowl IV "through the back door." Furthermore, Chiefs quarterback Len Dawson was an NFL washout. But he flourished in the AFL. Critics suggested that the lower level of play was the reason for his success. Then, five days before the game, Dawson was linked to a federal gambling investigation. He was cleared. Still, the anxiety he felt added to the pressure of preparing for the game. "It was, beyond a doubt, the toughest week of my life," he said later. Nevertheless, Kansas City had its own weapons. Three running backs combined for nearly 2,000 yards. The defensive line didn't have a nickname. But tackles Buck Buchanan and Curley Culp would have starred on any NFL team.

After the game began, the crowd was shocked. Kicker Jan Stenerud booted three field goals, giving Kansas City

GRIDIRON GREATS ∨
HAIL TO THE CHIEF

Kansas City mayor H. Roe Bartle was the chief executive of area Boy Scouts. He was nicknamed "The Chief." Physically, Bartle *looked* like a chief. He stood 6-foot-3 and weighed more than 300 pounds. He heard that Lamar Hunt wanted to relocate the Texans. Bartle invited Hunt to Kansas City. Hunt wasn't interested. Bartle didn't give up. He promised to sell 35,000 season tickets. He would enlarge Municipal Stadium, too. "Bartle did a remarkable selling job on Lamar Hunt," sports columnist Joe McGuff said, "and had it not been for his persuasiveness Hunt unquestionably would have taken his team elsewhere." Many fans wanted to honor Bartle. They suggested using his "Chief" nickname for the team. Hunt agreed.

DAWSON
16
LEN DAWSON

a 9–0 lead. Then the Chiefs recovered a fumbled Vikings kickoff. Running back Mike Garrett plunged into the end zone for the touchdown. Kansas City held a 16-point halftime lead. The Vikings scored near the end of the third quarter. But Dawson hit Otis Taylor with a short pass. The receiver high-stepped to a 46-yard touchdown. The Chiefs' victory was sealed. Dawson was named Most Valuable Player (MVP) of the game. "Our game plan wasn't very complicated," he said. "It involved throwing a lot of formations at them—formations they hadn't seen during the course of the season." Kansas City's defense halted the Vikings' running game. Minnesota recorded just 67 yards on the ground. "It was obvious that their offense had never seen a defense like ours," Dawson said.

GRIDIRON GREATS
A TRUE SPORTSMAN

As a child, Lamar Hunt was called "Games." He was always making up new sports. In college, he was a reserve tight end. He went on to extend his reach beyond football. He created a tennis league (World Championship Tennis). He was part-owner of the National Basketball Association's Chicago Bulls. He owned the minor-league baseball Dallas–Fort Worth Spurs. He also jump-started soccer in the United States. He helped found the North American Soccer League (NASL). The NASL folded. But Hunt was persistent. He helped found Major League Soccer (MLS) in 1993. He also owned three MLS teams. The Lamar Hunt Open Cup is the oldest continuously operating national soccer championship in the U.S.

47

2

RUNNING BACK ABNER HAYNES

OFF TO A GOOD START

n the late 1950s, Texas millionaire Lamar Hunt wanted an NFL team. It would play in his home city of Dallas. But the NFL turned him down. So Hunt decided to create his own league. He and several other wealthy men formed the AFL in 1960. It had eight teams. Hunt named his team the Texans. He wanted to appeal to the entire state.

To compete for fans, the NFL created the Dallas Cowboys. The Texans had trouble drawing fans. But those who showed up were treated to the thrilling performance of Abner

BOBBY BELL (NUMBER 78)

Haynes. He was the first in a long line of great running backs. In 1960, he led the AFL in rushing yards. He caught 55 passes, too. He earned both Rookie of the Year and Player of the Year awards.

In 1962, the Texans added Dawson. He hadn't played much in the NFL. Dallas gave him a fresh start. He led the team to the AFL Championship Game. Dallas beat the Houston Oilers in overtime. "There is no passer in professional football more accurate than Lenny," said coach Hank Stram.

Despite the win, Hunt decided that Dallas wasn't big enough for two teams. He wanted to move before the 1963 season. He considered Miami, Florida, and Atlanta, Georgia. But Kansas City, Missouri, mayor H. Roe Bartle made a great offer. Hunt decided to move there. The team became the Chiefs. They were mediocre at first. They finished 5–7–2 in 1963 and 7–7 in 1964.

In 1965, the Chiefs bolstered their offense. They drafted Otis Taylor. He had size, speed, strength, and agility. He also had confidence. "I'll tell you something about Otis Taylor," he said of himself. "He wants to be the best— always. There hasn't been a year when he didn't want to score more touchdowns than anybody and gain more yardage than anybody."

In 1966, linebackers Bobby Bell and E. J. Holub helped power the Chiefs past the Buffalo Bills in the AFL Championship Game. In previous seasons, that would have been the top accomplishment. But Hunt had been in talks with the NFL. The two leagues were planning to merge.

OTIS TAYLOR

GRIDIRON GREATS

SUPER BALL TO SUPER BOWL

Lamar Hunt didn't like the title "AFL–NFL World Championship Game." It was too long. But he didn't know what else to call it. During an owners meeting in 1966, he tried to reference the game. The term "Super Bowl" slipped out. Most owners liked it. They thought it was short and snappy. "It probably registered in my head because my daughter, Sharron, and my son, Lamar Jr., had a children's toy called a Super Ball," Hunt explained. "I probably interchanged the phonetics of 'bowl' and 'ball.'" In a note to the NFL commissioner, Hunt suggested adding Roman numerals. He thought it would give the game "more dignity."

"THERE IS NO PASSER IN PROFESSIONAL FOOTBALL MORE ACCURATE THAN LENNY."

—COACH HANK STRAM

The first step was a game between the champions of each league. This game soon became known as the Super Bowl. The Packers thumped the Chiefs in Super Bowl I.

Three years later, the Chiefs defeated the Oakland Raiders in the AFL championship. It was the final game in AFL history. The Chiefs finished the season on a high note. They defeated the Vikings in Super Bowl IV. From now on, both leagues would be part of the NFL. The Chiefs became part of the American Football Conference (AFC). In 1971, they met the Miami Dolphins in an epic playoff game. The Dolphins' Garo Yepremian kicked the winning field goal in the second overtime. The Chiefs suffered a heartbreaking 27–24 loss. The game lasted 82 minutes and 40 seconds. It is still the longest in NFL history.

LEN DAWSON
16

A PERIOD OF DECLINE

That game marked the end of an era. Next came a long period of mostly losing seasons. The team hit rock bottom in 1977. The Chiefs won just two games. They climbed to 8–8 in 1980. In 1981, they drafted running back Joe Delaney. At 5-foot-10 and 184 pounds, Delaney was small in stature. But he had quick feet and a big heart. Delaney galloped 1,121 yards that season. He earned AFC Rookie of the Year honors. The Chiefs improved to 9–7. It was their first winning mark in eight years. Tragedy struck on June 29, 1983. Delaney died while trying to save three boys from drowning. "When those little kids needed

ACTIONS SPEAK LOUDER THAN WORDS

During his five years in the NFL, Len Dawson started only two games. He threw just 45 passes. Texans' coach Hank Stram had coached Dawson at Purdue University. He invited Dawson to Dallas. Dawson led the team to the AFL championship in his first season. He earned the nickname "Lenny the Cool." At game time, he was calm and composed. He had a reserved personality off the field, too. "He could say more with a stare than most players could with words," said running back Ed Podolak. "He was the team leader, no doubt about it." Dawson compiled impressive statistics. But for him, it was not about the numbers. He focused on winning.

LEN DAWSON
QUARTERBACK
TEXANS/CHIEFS SEASONS: 1962–75
HEIGHT: 6 FEET
WEIGHT: 190 POUNDS
KANSAS CITY CHIEFS

help, he gave up his life trying to save them," said guard Tom Condon. "He wasn't a swimmer.... The man had a tremendous heart—he was special."

By 1986, Kansas City was a contender again. Much of its success was due to special-teams play. The team finished at 10–6. It made the postseason for the first time in 15 years. But it lost to the Jets, 35–15. Hunt shook up the franchise in late December 1988. Marty Schottenheimer was hired as coach. "I believe the opportunity is there with this football team to once again approach that great tradition of the Kansas City Chiefs," said Schottenheimer. He installed "Marty Ball," which focused on running the ball. His offense featured Christian Okoye. Okoye was a bruising running back. His nickname was "Nigerian Nightmare." Okoye led the Chiefs in rushing for four seasons. He set a team record in 1989 with 1,480 yards. That year also saw the rise of young defensive talent. One standout was aggressive linebacker Derrick Thomas.

DEFENSIVE END NEIL SMITH

The Chiefs' 11–5 mark in 1990 ushered them into the playoffs. They faced the Dolphins. Kansas City carried a 16–3 lead into the fourth quarter. But two Miami touchdowns led to a devastating 17–16 defeat. The next year, Kansas City met the Los Angeles Raiders in the postseason. The Chiefs won, 10–6. It was their first playoff victory in 22 years. But Buffalo ended their season the following week. In 1992, the Chiefs were back in the playoffs. This time, the San Diego Chargers crushed them.

After that, the Chiefs added two veterans: quarterback Joe Montana and running back Marcus Allen. They led the Chiefs to the AFC West Division title in 1993. They won two close playoff games. Then, they moved on to their first-ever AFC Championship Game. The Bills pulled away to win. The Chiefs matched up against Miami in the playoffs the following year. The game featured two of the league's best quarterbacks—Montana and Dan Marino. The Dolphins won, 27–17. Montana retired.

GRIDIRON GREATS

GETTING HIS KICKS

Jan Stenerud attended Montana State University in the 1960s. He had a skiing scholarship. The college's basketball coach saw him booming footballs "soccer style." The basketball coach contacted football coach Jim Sweeney. "[Sweeney] saw me a couple of weeks later running the stadium steps," Stenerud recalled, "and shouted, 'I hear you can kick.'" He could indeed. Stenerud starred for the next two years. He booted a 59-yard field goal. At the time, it was a collegiate record. He wasn't pro football's first soccer-style kicker. But he was arguably the best. When he retired, he ranked second in all-time scoring. Later, he became the first pure placekicker in the Hall of Fame.

373 CAREER FIELD GOALS MADE
558 CAREER FIELD GOALS ATTEMPTED

PRIEST HOLMES

WAY UP AND WAY DOWN

The Chiefs reloaded in 1995. They compiled a 13–3 record. It was the best in the NFL. But they stumbled in the playoffs. The offense turned over the ball four times in a loss to the Indianapolis Colts. Kansas City added running back Priest Holmes in 2001. He became the first undrafted free agent to lead the league in rushing. He did even better in 2002. Holmes ran wild behind tackle Willie Roaf and guard Brian Waters. They formed the dominant left side of one of the league's best offensive lines. Holmes led the Chiefs with 70 receptions. He tallied 2,287 total yards and

24 touchdowns to top the NFL. He was named Offensive Player of the Year. "He is doing stuff that has never been done in the history of the NFL, especially with those touchdowns," said tight end Tony Gonzalez.

In 2003, the Chiefs' offense was even better. They scored a franchise-record 484 points. Holmes rolled up an NFL-record 27 touchdowns. The high-powered Chiefs went 13–3. They topped the AFC West. They hosted the Colts in the playoffs. The game was an offensive shootout. Holmes ran for 176 yards and 2 touchdowns. Still, the Chiefs were outgunned, 38–31. The following season, their defense struggled. Kansas City dropped to a disappointing 7–9 record.

Partway through the 2005 season, Holmes suffered a serious injury. It would lead to the end of his career. His backup was Larry Johnson. He impressed fans as he plowed through defenders. The Chiefs improved to 10–6. They narrowly missed the playoffs. In 2006, the offense focused on Johnson. He made an NFL-record 416 rushing attempts. Johnson's effort boosted the Chiefs back into the postseason. But once again, they were stopped by Indianapolis.

Kansas City plummeted to 4–12 in 2007. The year ended with nine straight losses. "We're underachievers," said Gonzalez after the season. "It's embarrassing. It's frustrating. I think it's ridiculous. We're one of the worst teams in the NFL, record-wise. That's something I never thought would happen out here in Kansas City."

It kept happening. The team plunged to 2–14 in 2008. It went 4–12 the following year. Running back Jamaal Charles was a rare bright spot. In the final game of the 2009 season, he set a team record with 259 rushing yards.

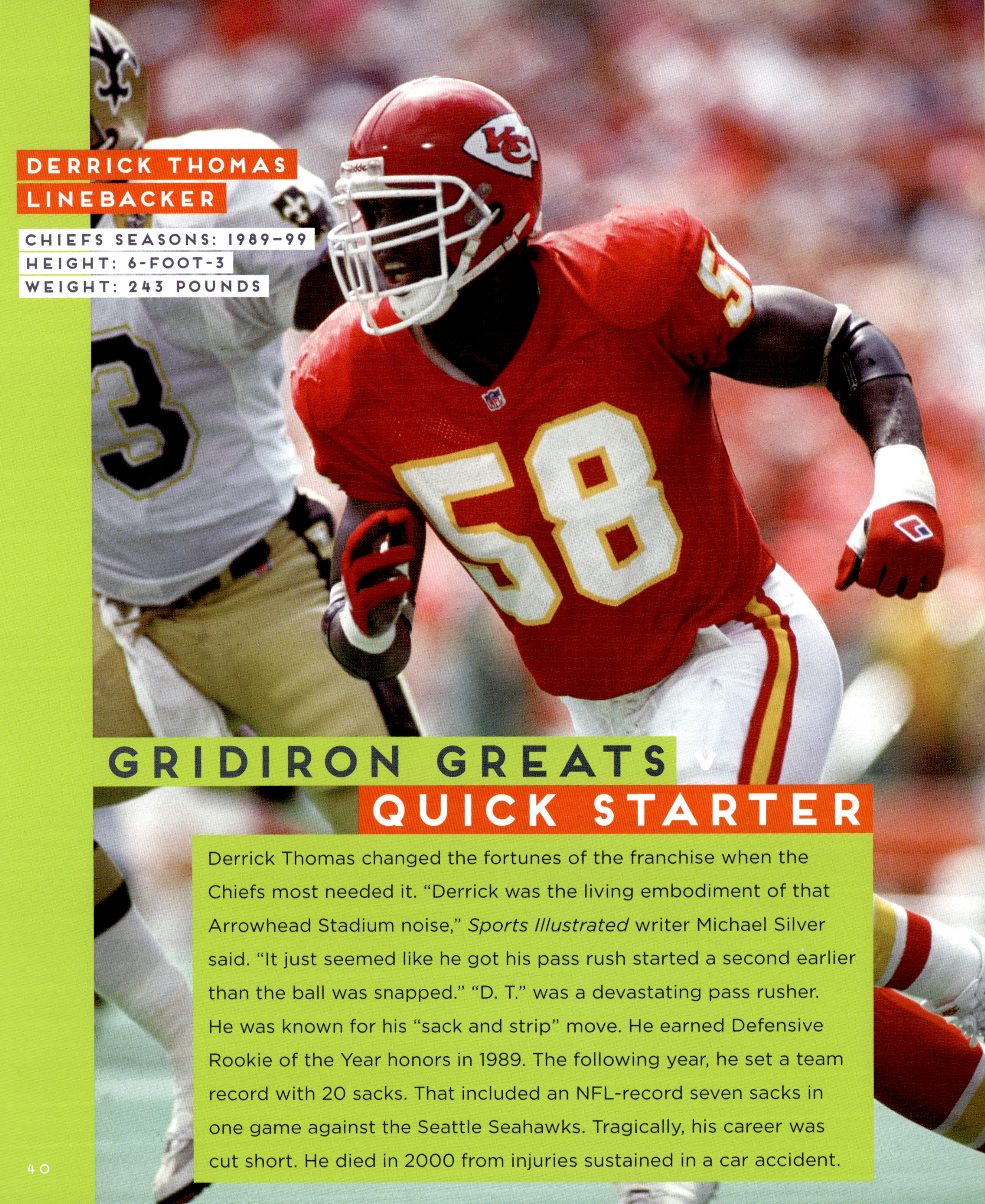

GRIDIRON GREATS

QUICK STARTER

Derrick Thomas changed the fortunes of the franchise when the Chiefs most needed it. "Derrick was the living embodiment of that Arrowhead Stadium noise," *Sports Illustrated* writer Michael Silver said. "It just seemed like he got his pass rush started a second earlier than the ball was snapped." "D. T." was a devastating pass rusher. He was known for his "sack and strip" move. He earned Defensive Rookie of the Year honors in 1989. The following year, he set a team record with 20 sacks. That included an NFL-record seven sacks in one game against the Seattle Seahawks. Tragically, his career was cut short. He died in 2000 from injuries sustained in a car accident.

126.5

169

BOUNCING BACK

The Chiefs bounced back in 2010. Quarterback Matt Cassel tossed 27 touchdown passes. Charles averaged more than six yards per carry. He tallied 1,467 rushing yards. These individual performances contributed to a respectable 10–6 record. In the postseason, the Chiefs were squashed by the Baltimore Ravens. The 2011 campaign got off to a rocky start. Kansas City dropped its first three games. Charles suffered a season-ending knee injury. The Chiefs slid to 7–9. Still, Kansas City remained optimistic that Cassel and Charles would revive the offense.

That optimism crumbled in 2012. Kansas City limped through the season with just two wins. The team hired coach Andy Reid to turn things around. Behind quarterback Alex Smith, Kansas City opened 2013 with a nine-game winning streak. The Chiefs finished 11–5. They put the "wild" in the Wild Card round of the playoffs. In the third quarter, the Chiefs led the Colts by 28 points. But they couldn't hold on. The Colts galloped back to win, 45–44. The Chiefs dipped to 9–7 in 2014. They returned to the playoffs in 2015 with an 11–5 mark. But a 27–20 loss to the New England Patriots ended their season.

Kansas City's 12–4 mark in 2016 was its best in 13 years. But the Chiefs fell victim to the Steelers. Pittsburgh became the first team in nearly a decade to win a playoff game without scoring a touchdown. It had six field goals in an 18–16 win. In 2017, the Chiefs suffered another narrow playoff loss. During the Wild Card game, the Chiefs led the Tennessee Titans 21–3 at halftime. But they sputtered in the second half. Tennessee pulled out a 22–21 win. After the season, the Chiefs traded Smith.

LINEBACKER DEE FORD

That opened the door for Patrick Mahomes to take over as the team's on-field leader. He was the Chiefs' top draft pick in 2017. Mahomes led Kansas City to a 12–4 record in 2018. The Chiefs charged into the playoffs but dropped the AFC championship to the Patriots in an overtime loss.

From the team's beginning as Lamar Hunt's "Plan B," it has played a major role in shaping the modern NFL. The Chiefs' history includes an appearance in the first Super Bowl. It also boasts an upset victory in Super Bowl IV. That win proved the AFL could produce worthy opponents. Now, the Kansas City Chiefs are intent on adding more accolades to their rich history.

AFL CHAMPIONSHIPS

1962, 1969

WEBSITES

KANSAS CITY CHIEFS

https://www.chiefs.com/

NFL: KANSAS CITY CHIEFS TEAM PAGE

http://www.nfl.com/teams/kansascitychiefs/profile?team=KC

INDEX

DERRICK THOMAS